T0053461

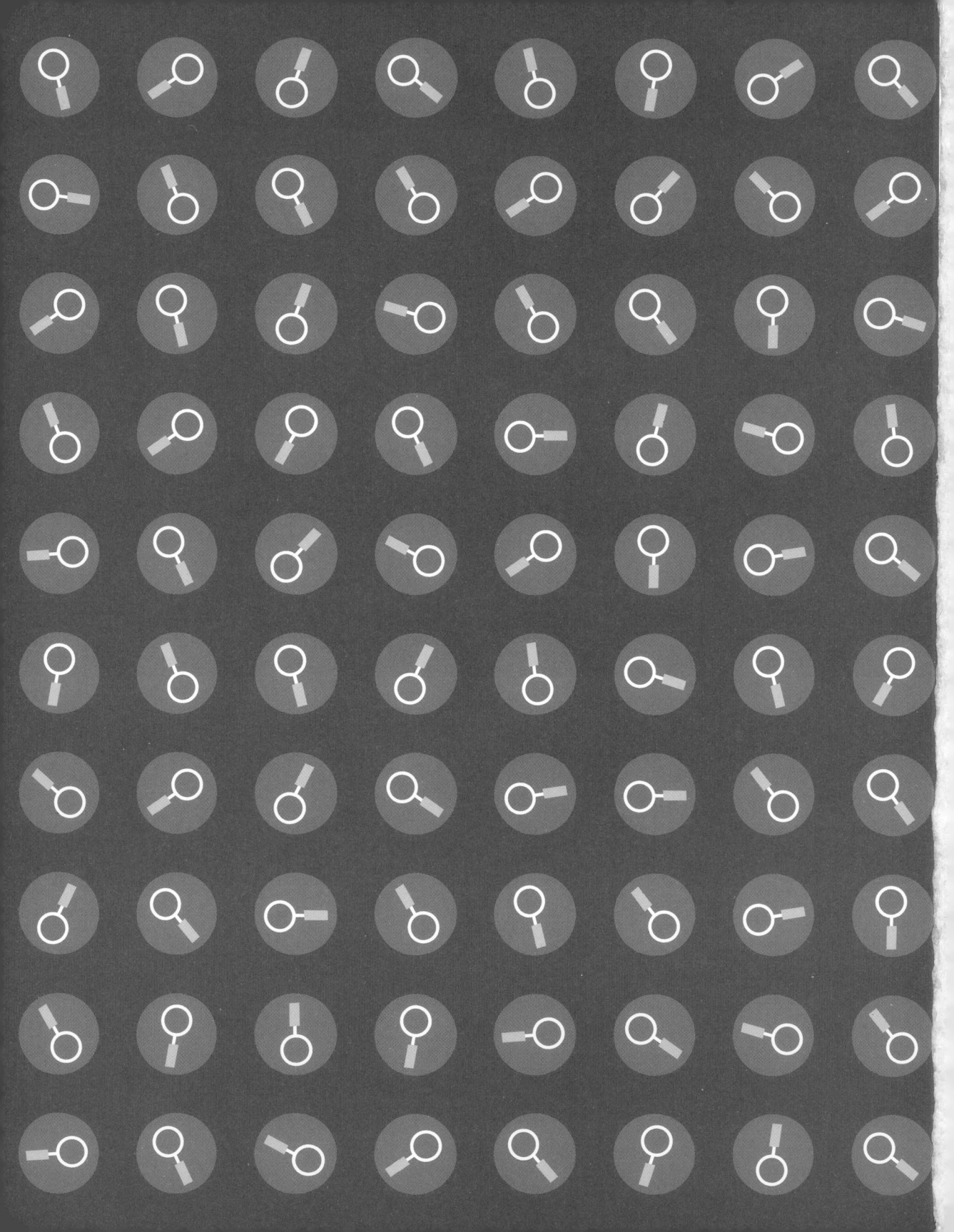

Spot the Differences

AROUND THE WORLD

By Sarah Parvis and Georgia Rucker

PBS KIDS and the PBS KIDS logo are registered marks of the Public Broadcasting Service. Used with permission. © 2019 PBS. All rights reserved.

100% of the net proceeds PBS KIDS receives from your purchase of this book supports the mission of PBS.

www.pbskids.org

downtown bookworks

Downtown Bookworks Inc.
265 Canal Street, New York, NY 10013

Copyright © 2019 by Downtown Bookworks Inc.

By Sarah Parvis
Designed by Georgia Rucker
Printed in China, June 2019

10 9 8 7 6 5 4 3 2 1

All rights reserved. No part of this book may be reproduced in any form or by any means without prior written permission from the publisher.

PHOTO CREDITS Front cover: ©iStock.com/coramueller (bear), photopixel/Shutterstock.com (flags), Africa Studio/Shutterstock.com (balloons), FeellFree/Shutterstock.com (sunglasses), ©iStock.com/RASimon (beach ball). Interior: 1: CECIL BO DZWOWA/Shutterstock.com (boys), BaLL LunLa/Shutterstock.com (remote), olegganko/Shutterstock.com (yellow bar), Roman Samborskyi/Shutterstock.com (medal), Alexei Zatevakhin/Shutterstock.com (mallets). 3: Natalia Barsukova/Shutterstock.com (flamingos), Oleksii Lomako/Shutterstock.com (float), Africa Studio/Shutterstock.com (necklace). 4: Song_about_summer/Shutterstock.com (Antarctica), untitled/Shutterstock.com (float), oobqoo/Shutterstock.com (ripped jeans), ©iStock.com/RyanJLane (fanny pack). 5: Dietmar Temps/Shutterstock.com (Madagascar), WilleeCole Photography/Shutterstock.com (glasses), ChiccoDodiFC/Shutterstock.com (weather vane). 6: Alexey Fedorenko/Shutterstock.com (Scotland, flag), Weho/Shutterstock.com (bear), New Africa/Shutterstock.com (fingers). 7: Benny Marty/Shutterstock.com (Greece), Jakkrit Orrasri/Shutterstock.com (bone), otsphoto/Shutterstock.com (leash), Dimitrios/Shutterstock.com (statue). 8: ©iStock.com/swissmediavision (New Zealand, new legs), Cherdchai charasri/Shutterstock.com (basketball), Doug Lemke/Shutterstock.com (lighthouse), Alex Bard/Shutterstock.com (tail). 9: muratart/Shutterstock.com (Turkey), Lizard/Shutterstock.com (flag), Elena Rostunova/Shuttertstock.com (turret), Thye-Wee Gn/Shutterstock.com (chairs), Mrs_ya/Shutterstock.com (red carpet). 10: Ko Backpacko/Shutterstock.com (Myanmar), vander/Shutterstock.com (clock), donatas1205/Shutterstock.com (buttons), Roman Samokhin/Shutterstock.com (watermelon), asharkyu/Shutterstock.com (ivy). 11: Natalia Kirichenko/Shutterstock.com (Australia), Valentina Razumova/Shutterstock.com (carrot). 12: CroMary/Shutterstock.com (Netherlands), Anna Maloverjan/Shutterstock.com (ponytail), Butterfly Hunter/Shutterstock.com (butterfly), Hekla/Shutterstock.com (hand), Dmitry Zimin/Shutterstock.com (umbrella). 13: Deborah Augsburger/Shutterstock.com (Bolivia), stifos/Shutterstock.com (llama sign), Byelikova Oksana/Shutterstock.com (cactus), Krasowit/Shutterstock.com (fish), Africa Studio/Shutterstock.com (scarf). 14: Marvin Minder/Shutterstock.com (Costa Rica, new sloth), StudioSmart/Shutterstock.com (bear), Evdokimov Maxim/Shutterstock.com (bow). 15: Arsenie Krasnevsky/Shutterstock.com (France), photomaster/Shutterstock.com (falcon), OrangeGroup/Shutterstock.com (pant leg), railway fx/Shutterstock.com (flag). 16: Vixit/Shutterstock.com (Maldives, flip-flops), Baanrukbua/Shutterstock.com (coconuts), RUTiAM/Shutterstock.com (bear). 17: MikeDotta/Shutterstock.com (Egypt), topseller/Shutterstock.com (hot-air balloon). 18: BlueOrange Studio/Shutterstock.com (Norway), Piotr Piatrouski/Shutterstock.com (igloo), Dzha33/Shutterstock.com (horn), Irina Rogova/Shutterstock.com (tree). 19: Sun_Shine/Shutterstock.com (Tanzania), S_Photo/Shutterstock.com (sand art), Vereshchagin Dmitry/Shutterstock.com (sail), Kues/Shutterstock.com (scales), Ruth Black/Shutterstock.com (lollipop). 20: MinhHue/Shutterstock.com (all). 21: SvetlanaSF/Shutterstock.com (Bahamas), Calvste/Shutterstock.com (feathers), Eric Isselee/Shutterstock.com (chipmunk). 22: Olexandr Taranukhin/Shutterstock.com (Ukraine), ekapol sirachainan/Shutterstock.com (keyboard), goir/Shutterstock.com (sign), Mark_KA/Shutterstock.com (cat), Iasha/Shutterstock.com (bat). 23: lunamarina/Shutterstock.com (Mexico), Nuttapong/Shutterstock.com (hat), Dmitry Rukhlenko/Shutterstock.com (blue statue). 24: Chrispictures/Shutterstock.com (Colombia), Amam ka/Shutterstock.com (soccer balls). 25: ©iStock.com/filipefrazao (Brazil), pukach/Shutterstock.com (balloon), Ruslan Kudrin/Shutterstock.com (flower). 26: Wutthichai/Shutterstock.com (Thailand), april70/Shutterstock.com (new flower), Ekkoss/Shutterstock.com (cactus), saravutpics/Shutterstock.com (pillar). 27: Anna Jedynak/Shutterstock.com (Cuba), Cameris/Shutterstock.com (signal), Sabino Parente/Shutterstock.com (flag). 28: PawelG Photo/Shutterstock.com (Germany), George3973/Shutterstock.com (hard pretzel), rayjunk/Shutterstock.com (mustard). 29: Grigvovan/Shutterstock.com (Iran), Veniamin Kraskov/Shutterstock.com (watering can, pinwheel), canbedone/Shutterstock.com (doll), design56/Shutterstock.com (backpack). 30–31: Max Topchii/Shutterstock.com. 31: Suzanne Tucker/Shutterstock.com (eyeballs), muratart/Shutterstock.com (dolphins), visionaryft/Shutterstock.com (flippers). 32: Hung Chung Chih/Shutterstock.com (China), Diego Gutierrez Yrizar/Shutterstock.com (streetlight), LUMPANG MOONMUANG/Shutterstock.com (glove), Mega Pixel/Shutterstock.com (peace sign), VAV/Shutterstock.com (chalk). 33: SL-Photography/Shutterstock.com (Peru, new head), Serge Siro/Shutterstock.com (wall). 34: norikko/Shutterstock.com (Japan, soy sauce), Africa Studio/Shutterstock.com (chopsticks). 35: CECIL BO DZWOWA/Shutterstock.com (Zimbabwe), BaLL LunLa/Shutterstock.com (remote), olegganko/Shutterstock.com (yellow bar), Roman Samborskyi/Shutterstock.com (medal), Alexei Zatevakhin/Shutterstock.com (mallets). 36–37: Gilmanshin/Shutterstock.com. 37: Ruth Black/Shutterstock.com (cupcake), Dan Kosmayer/Shutterstock.com (chocolate), yukihipo/Shutterstock.com (birthday hat), defpicture/Shutterstock.com (window). 38: MarkLG/Shutterstock.com (all). 39: Quick Shot/Shutterstock.com (Mali), Richard Peterson/Shutterstock.com (ladder), Ljupco Smokovski/Shutterstock.com (seesaw), Heike Brauer/Shutterstock.com (cone). 40–41: SAPhotog/Shutterstock.com. 41: New Vibe/Shutterstock.com (flower), Taweesak Sriwannawit/Shutterstock.com (lantern). 42: Drop of Light/Shutterstock.com (Vatican City), terekhov igor/Shutterstock.com (broom), Anton Starikov/Shutterstock.com (pom-pom), Benjamin Miner/Shutterstock.com (toy soldier), TaraPatta/Shutterstock.com (door). 43: Amy Nichole Harris/Shutterstock.com (Chile), Anthony Booker/Shutterstock.com (new statue), Alberto Loyo/Shutterstock.com (boulder), SUPAPORNKH/Shutterstock.com (flowers), OSORIOartist/Shutterstock.com (horse). 44–45: Angela N Perryman/Shutterstock.com. 45: Chanita Chokchaikul/Shutterstock.com (bangs), Kate Pi/Shutterstock.com (flower). 46: Cynthia Liang/Shutterstock.com (England), Dan Kosmayer/Shutterstock.com (ice cream), Sanit Fuangnakhon/Shutterstock.com (tree). 47: ©iStock.com/hadynyah (India), vetre/Shutterstock.com (sandcastle), LifetimeStock/Shutterstock.com (fennec fox). 48–49: ziggy_mars/Shutterstock.com. 49: fewerton/Shutterstock.com (sunglasses), Akitameldes/Shutterstock.com (dog). 50: GuoZhongHua/Shutterstock.com (Cambodia), iFocus/Shutterstock.com (stuffed elephant), Chimpinski/Shutterstock.com (top hat), nasidastudio/Shutterstock.com (trunk), bergamont/Shutterstock.com (bananas). 51: chythaiphotocyber/Shutterstock.com (Switzerland), ragophotos/Shutterstock.com (cow), LightField Studios/Shutterstock.com (tool belt), elena_timiy/Shutterstock.com (goo), Aleksandar Grozdanovski/Shutterstock.com (valves), Photo Melon/Shutterstock.com (kite). 52: Aleksei Potov/Shutterstock.com (Canada), Checubus/Shutterstock.com (bear sign), Susan Schmitz/Shutterstock.com (dog), thechatat/Shutterstock.com (alligator), Iasha/Shutterstock.com (hockey stick), Smit/Shutterstock.com (tree). 53: David Steele/Shutterstock.com (UAE), Pixeljoy/Shutterstock.com pirate flag), Lilu330/Shutterstock.com (sticker), Erin Donalson/Shutterstock.com (whale tail). 54: Anton_Ivanov/Shutterstock.com (Ghana), mmalkani/Shutterstock.com (flower print), Punchalit Chotiksatian/Shutterstock.com (lei), Karkas/Shutterstock.com (purse). 55: Nokuro/Shutterstock.com (Malaysia), Gavran333/Shutterstock.com (new tongs), Bryan Solomon/Shutterstock.com (chocolate donut). 56: StockphotoVideo/Shutterstock.com (Latvia), Shvaygert Ekaterina/Shutterstoc.com (gum), Ukki Studio/Shutterstock.com (heart), Wuttichok Panichiwarapun/Shutterstock.com (ukulele), Nenad Nedomacki/Shutterstock.com (face paint). 57: FuGazi images/Shutterstock.com (Morocco), Andrei Kholmov/Shutterstock.com (pizza), LongQuattro/Shutterstock.com (tire tracks), Peter Turner Photography/Shutterstock.com (flower pot), MirasWonderland/Shutterstock.com (cat). Back cover: CroMary/Shutterstock.com (Netherlands), Anna Maloverjan/Shutterstock.com (ponytail), Butterfly Hunter/Shutterstock.com (butterfly), Hekla/Shutterstock.com (hand), Dmitry Zimin/Shutterstock.com (umbrella).

Spot the Differences

Look at each pair of pictures. Point at everything that is different. And count the differences you find.

Hi, parents! As your kids do these puzzles, tell them to look out for:

- **items that have appeared or disappeared**
- **things that have gotten larger or smaller or shorter or longer**
- **colors that have changed**
- **objects that have been replaced with something new**

If your child is stumped, remind them to look closely at each picture and how they are different.

You can even ask questions to help.
Are all of the trees the same?
Do all of the flamingoes' necks look the same?
Is there anything new in the water?

This number tells you how many differences are in the puzzle.

The puzzles get more challenging as you go!

Spot the differences puzzles are a great workout for visual observation and spatial relations skills. Encourage your child to celebrate each find by saying what they spotted aloud. Naming objects, colors, and size differences will also boost your child's vocabulary and confidence—plus, it's fun!

Cool Picture!

Point to **4** differences

Antarctica

Beautiful Boat by the Sea

Point to **4** differences

Madagascar

Playing Bagpipes

Point to **4** differences

Scotland

Rover Among the Ruins

Point to **4** differences

Greece

Boulders on the Beach

Point to **4** differences

New Zealand

Welcome to Topkapi Palace

Point to **4** differences

Turkey

Monks Play Ball Too!

Point to **4** differences

Myanmar

Hoppy Kangaroos

Point to **4** differences

Australia

Delightful Dutch Day

Point to **4** differences

The Netherlands

Llama Drama

Point to **4** differences

Bolivia

Baby Sloth

Point to **4** differences

Costa Rica

What a View!

Point to **4** differences

France

Island Time

Point to **4** differences

The Maldives

Camel Kisses

Point to **4** differences

Egypt

Reindeer Games

Point to **4** differences

Norway

Sun, Sand, and Scales

Point to **4** differences

Tanzania

Let's Play Catch!

Point to **4** differences

Vietnam

Music to My Ears

Point to **4** differences

The Bahamas

A Windy Day by the Mill

Point to **4** differences

Ukraine

Iguana's Day Out

Point to **4** differences

Mexico

Future Soccer Star

Point to **4** differences

Colombia

Let's Stroll!

Point to **4** differences

Brazil

A Cactus for the King!

Point to **4** differences

Thailand

Taxi! Taxi!

Point to **4** differences

Cuba

Pretzel Perfection

Point to **5** differences

Germany

School Friends

Point to **5** differences

Iran

Adventure Ahoy!

Point to **5** differences

Walking on the Great Wall

Point to **5** differences

China

Relaxing in a Row

Point to **5** differences

Peru

pan

Xylophone Practice

Point to **5** differences

Zimbabwe

St. Basil's Birthday Bash!

Point to **5** differences

Perfectly Pink

Point to **5** differences

Italy

An Amazing Mosque

Point to **5** differences

Mali

Don't Forget Your Lunch

Point to **5** differences

Tanzania

On Guard!

Point to **5** differences

Vatican City

A Visitor on Easter Island

Point to **5** differences

Chile

What a Doll!

Point to **5** differences

Ice Cream for the Queen!

Point to **5** differences

England

Desert Stroll

Point to **5** differences

India

Ready for School

Point to **6** differences

An Elephant Ride

Point to **6** differences

Cambodia

Alphorns in the Alps

Point to **6** differences

Switzerland

Big Jump!

Point to **6** differences

Canada

Sailboat Race

Point to **6** differences

United Arab Emirates

Say Hello as You Go

Point to **6** differences

Ghana

Snack Time!

Point to **6** differences

Malaysia

Make Some Noise

Point to **7** differences

Latvia

Watch Out!

Point to **7** differences

Morocco

Answer Key

front cover

p. 3

p. 4

p. 5

p. 6

p. 7

p. 8

p. 9

p. 10

p. 11

p. 12

p. 13

p. 14

p. 15

p. 16

Answer Key

p. 17

p. 18

p. 19

p. 20

p. 21

p. 22

p. 23

p. 24

p. 25

p. 26

p. 27

p. 28

p. 29

p. 30–31

p. 32

p. 33

Answer Key

p. 34

p. 35

p. 36–37

p. 38

p. 39

p. 40–41

p. 42

p. 43

p. 44–45

p. 46

p. 47

p. 48–49

p. 50

p. 51

p. 52

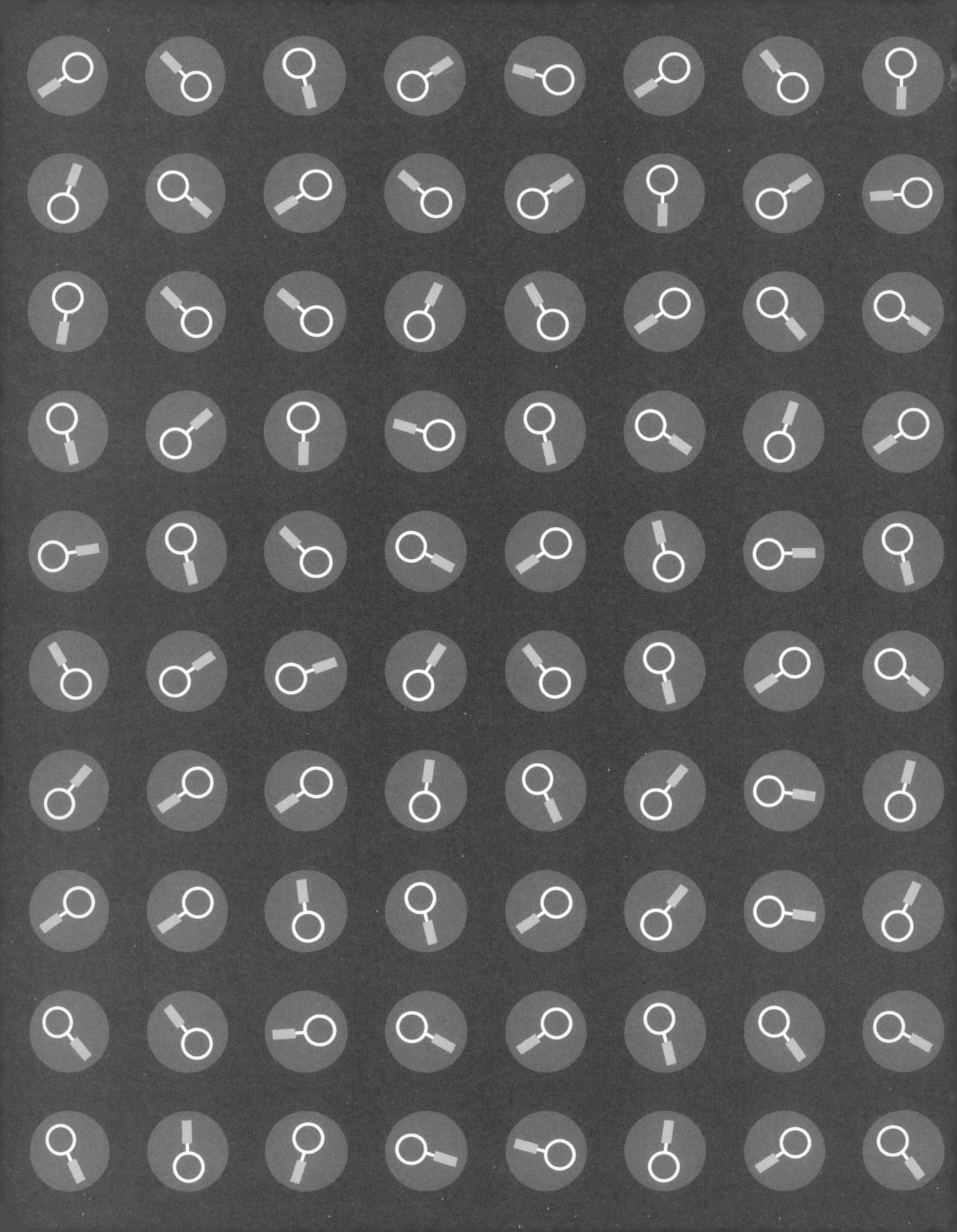